Romania Fun Facts Picture Book for Kids

An Educational City Travel Photography Photobook About History, Places with Everything You Need to Know About the Country for Children & Teens

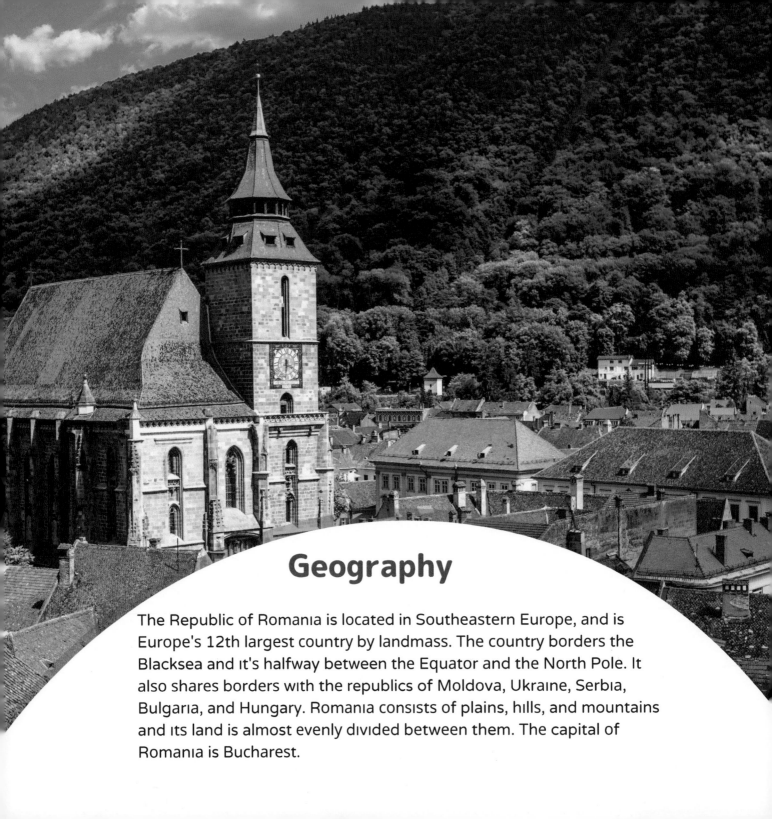

Geography

The Republic of Romania is located in Southeastern Europe, and is Europe's 12th largest country by landmass. The country borders the Blacksea and it's halfway between the Equator and the North Pole. It also shares borders with the republics of Moldova, Ukraine, Serbia, Bulgaria, and Hungary. Romania consists of plains, hills, and mountains and its land is almost evenly divided between them. The capital of Romania is Bucharest.

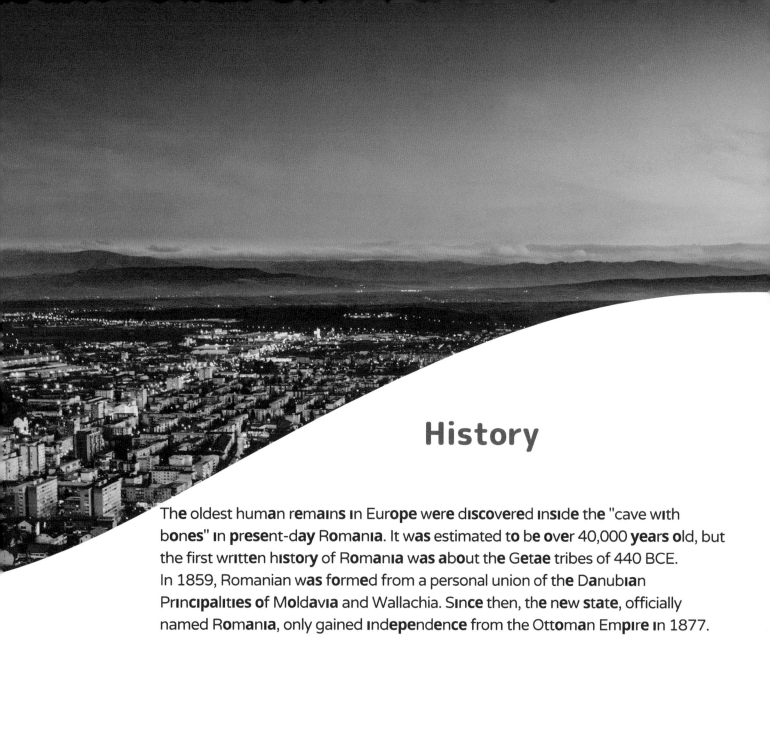

History

The oldest human remains in Europe were discovered inside the "cave with bones" in present-day Romania. It was estimated to be over 40,000 years old, but the first written history of Romania was about the Getae tribes of 440 BCE. In 1859, Romanian was formed from a personal union of the Danubian Principalities of Moldavia and Wallachia. Since then, the new state, officially named Romania, only gained independence from the Ottoman Empire in 1877.

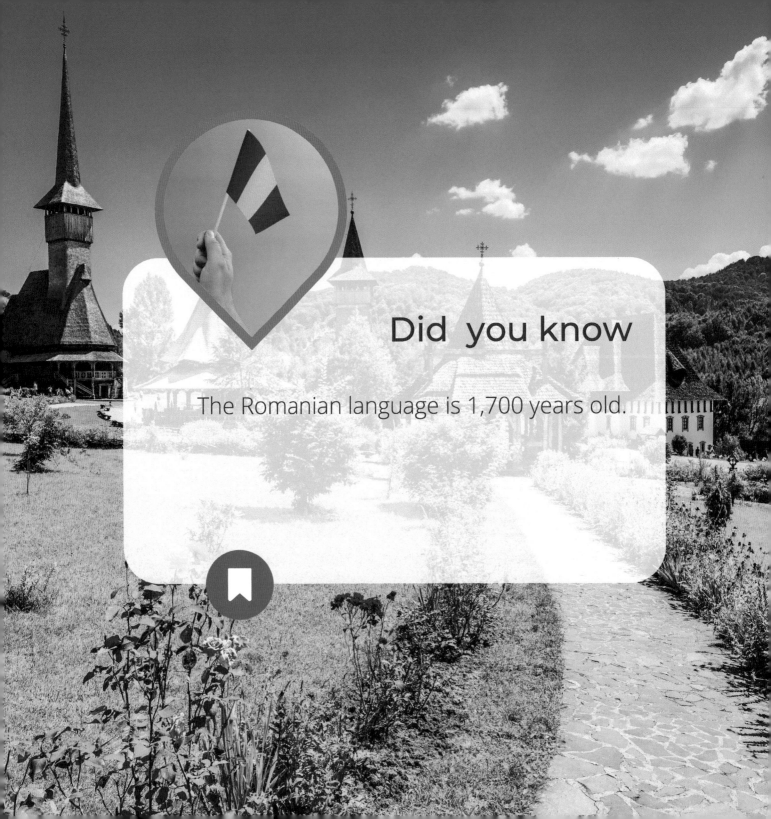

Did you know

The Romanian language is 1,700 years old.

Climate

The climate of Romania is continental, especially in the Old kingdom. Winter, summer, and autumn are the principal seasons in the country. Winters are always long and cold while the summers are hot. Rainfall is heaviest in April and lasts through till July.

People

Native Romanians are about 89% of the population. Hungarian, Gypsy, German, Armenian, Croatian, and Turkish are other minority ethnicities in the country. Most people in Romania are Christian, with Eastern Orthodox as the majority group. Others include Greek Catholic, Roman Catholic, Protestant, Unitarian, and Jewish.

Romanian is the native language. English, French, and German are common foreign languages. The literacy rate in the country is 98%.

Romanians are friendly and hospitable. They are playful, warm, and fun to be with.

Culture

The culture of Romania is rich and varied. Major elements of the culture include architecture, art, music, literature, cuisine, clothing, and folk traditions.

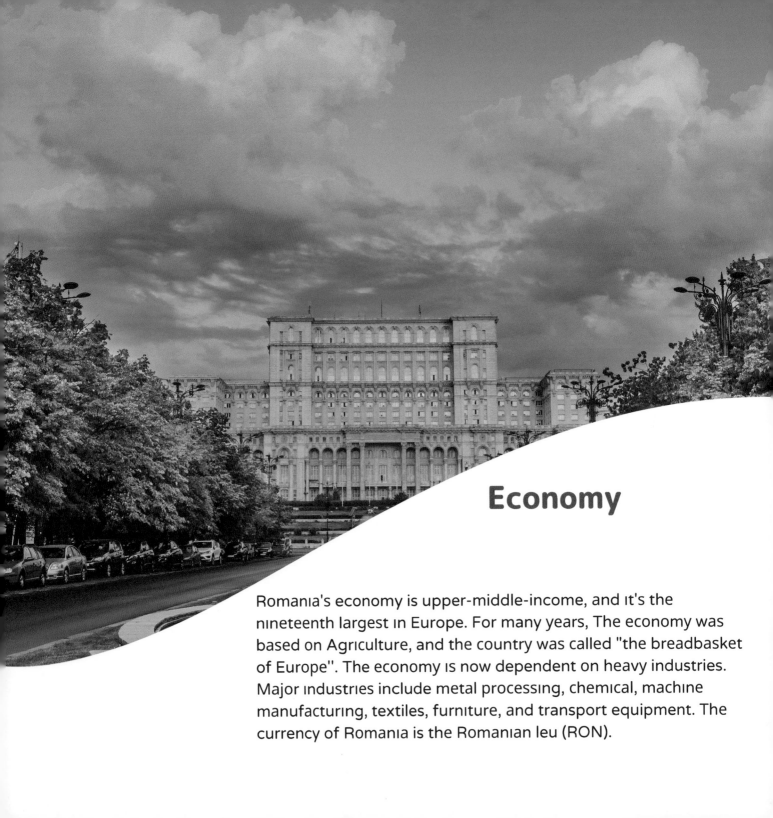

Economy

Romania's economy is upper-middle-income, and it's the nineteenth largest in Europe. For many years, The economy was based on Agriculture, and the country was called "the breadbasket of Europe". The economy is now dependent on heavy industries. Major industries include metal processing, chemical, machine manufacturing, textiles, furniture, and transport equipment. The currency of Romania is the Romanian leu (RON).

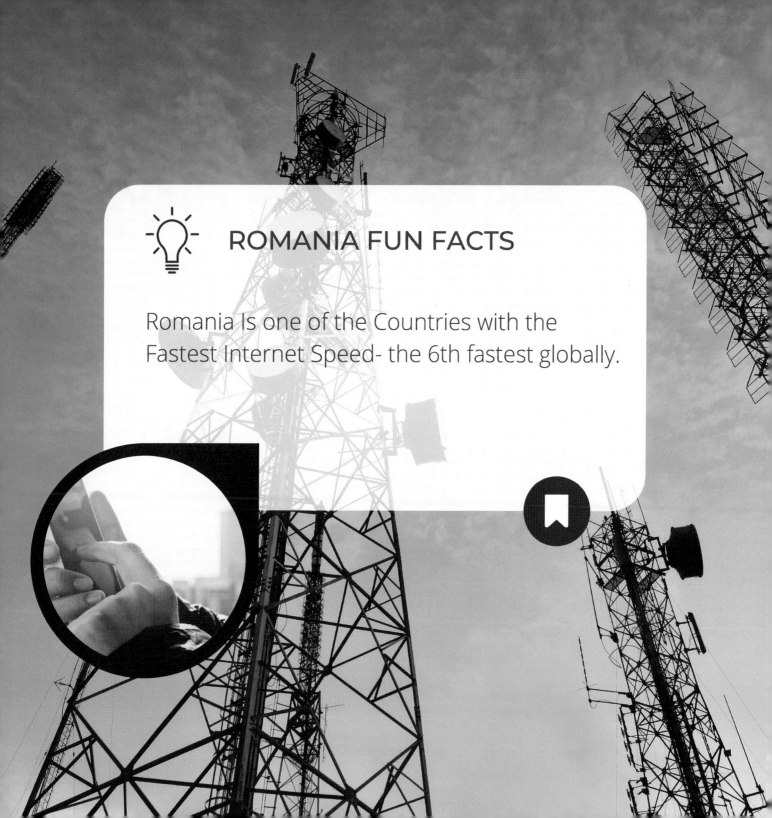

ROMANIA FUN FACTS

Romania Is one of the Countries with the Fastest Internet Speed- the 6th fastest globally.

Public Holidays

Most of the holidays in Romania vary from year to year. Below are popular national holidays.

New Year Holiday- Jan 1-2
Union Day-Jan 24
Constantin Brancusi- Feb 19
Orthodox Good Friday-
Orthodox Easter Monday
Labor Day-May 1st
Whit Monday
Children's Day-June 1st
Assumption of Mary- Aug 15
Saint Andrew Day-Nov 30
National Day-Dec 1st
Christmas Holidays

Tourist attractions

Whether you are visiting Romania for the first time or coming for a special occasion, you'll find a country full of impressive landmarks and exciting things to do.

Bran Castle

The castle is often associated with Dracula's home. The castle has a root dating back to the 13th century. Presently, it's a museum displaying art and furniture collected by Queen Maria. It also contains an open-air museum that features Romanian peasant buildings.

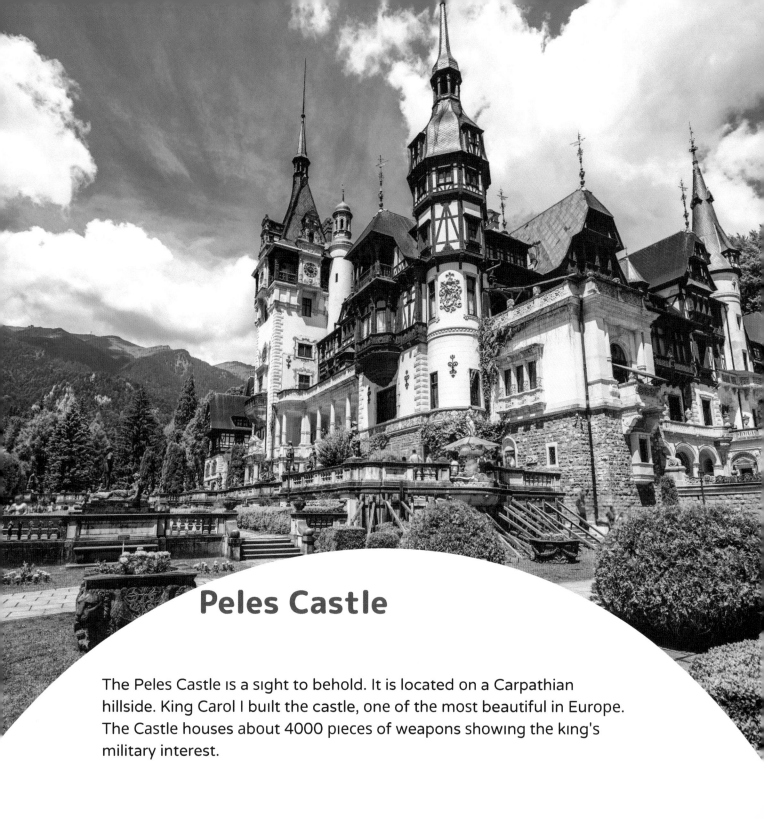

Peles Castle

The Peles Castle is a sight to behold. It is located on a Carpathian hillside. King Carol I built the castle, one of the most beautiful in Europe. The Castle houses about 4000 pieces of weapons showing the king's military interest.

ROMANIA FUN FACTS

Romania has the first electrified castle in Europe. Peleș castle became the world's first castle fully powered by locally produced electricity.

The Palace Of Parliament

This palace is the biggest and probably the heaviest administrative building in the world used for civilian purposes. It's the second-largest administration building in the world, only behind the Pentagon. It's home to the Romanian Senate and the Romanian Chamber of Deputies.

ROMANIA FUN FACTS

The Palace of the Parliament is the heaviest building in the world, weighing about 4,098,500,000 kilograms (9.04 billion pounds; 4.10 million tonnes)

The Old Town

The old town is locally called Centru Vechi. It is located in the center of the city of Bucharest. The town was once a necessary stop along the trading route from the Ottoman Empire to Leipzig. It was devastated by many unfortunate situations, including WWII, and it's now only about 20% of what it used to be but still houses many attractions to see.

Brasov

Brasov is Romania's 7th most populous city. The city is filled with baroque, gothic, and renaissance buildings and historical attractions, including the black church.

Râșnov Citadel

Râșnov Citadel is a big mountain fort built as a defense against the outer borders of the historic Hungarian empire. It is located at the mouth of the Bran Pass. The citadel is enormous and holds many historical moments begging to be explored

Romania fun facts

Bucharest is called "Little Paris." The city's Arcul de Triumf was constructed in 1935 to be modeled after the Arc de Triomphe in Paris.

Festivals

Romanians celebrate their history, heritage, and seasons annually and unchanged festivals annually. Some of the popular festivals include;

Popular annual events and festivals

Wine Festivals- Annual October festival is usually held in winemaking areas of Romania to celebrate the beginning of the grape harvest.

Untold Festival-Romania's annual largest music festival in the city of Cluj Napoca.

Romania International Shakespeare Festival - June festival that takes place every 2 years in Craiova to celebrate English playwrights.

Bucharest International Jazz Competition - 7 days annual Jazz festival in May in Bucharest that gathers bands from Europe, Asia, North America, and South America.

Transylvania International Film Festival (TIFF) is Romania's largest international film festival. It's for promoting cinematic art

Museums

Romania has some of the most important museums in the world, and it would be wrong not to visit at least one.

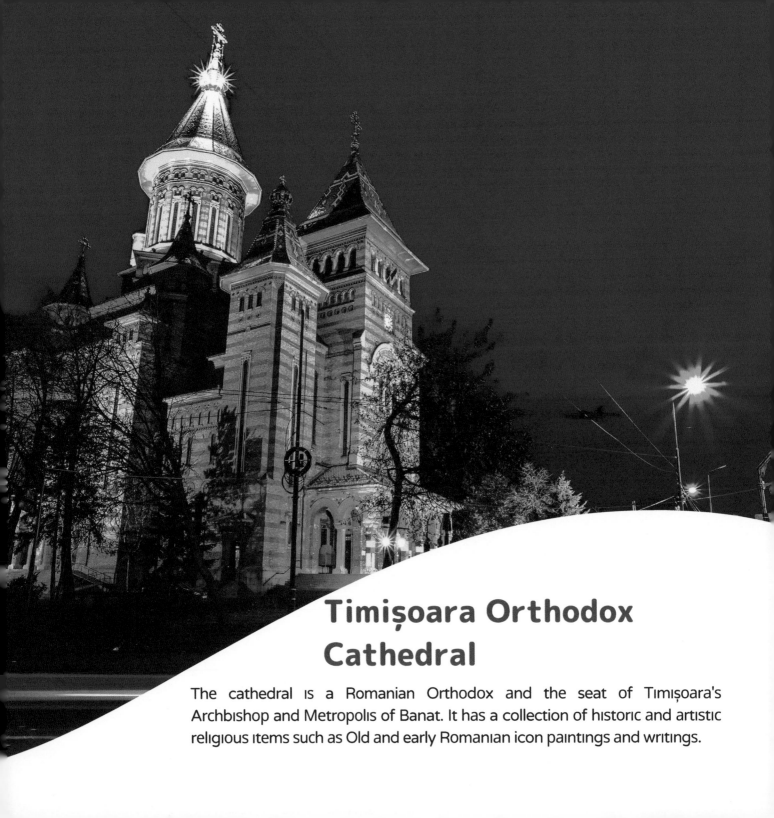

Timișoara Orthodox Cathedral

The cathedral is a Romanian Orthodox and the seat of Timișoara's Archbishop and Metropolis of Banat. It has a collection of historic and artistic religious items such as Old and early Romanian icon paintings and writings.

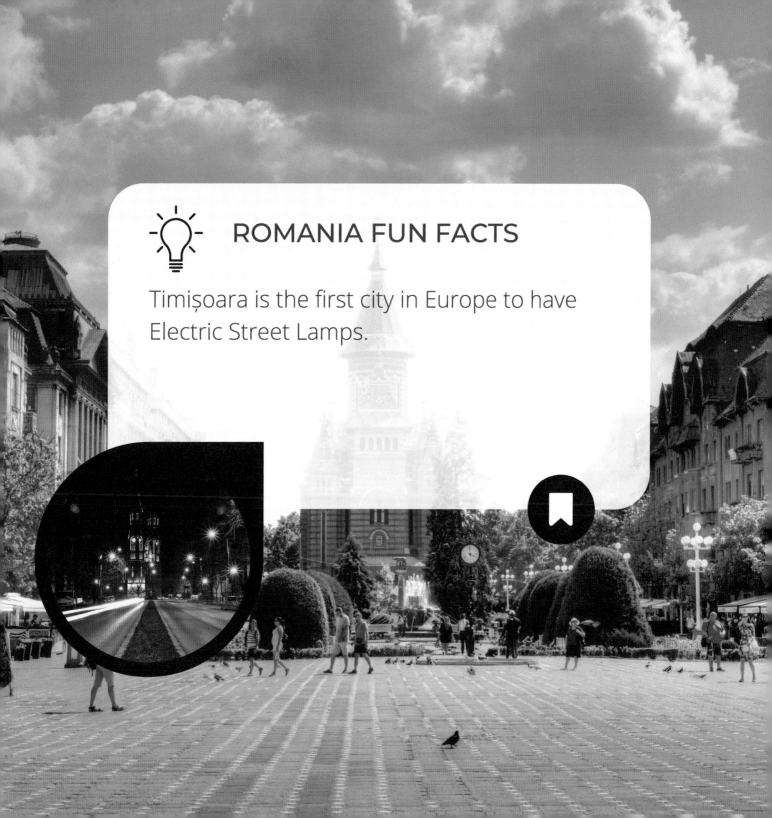

ROMANIA FUN FACTS

Timișoara is the first city in Europe to have Electric Street Lamps.

Grigore Antipa National Museum of Natural History

The Museum is located in Bucharest and contains different natural history collections such as Geological Collections, Anatomy Collections, Paleontology Collections, and Ethnographic and Anthropological Collections.

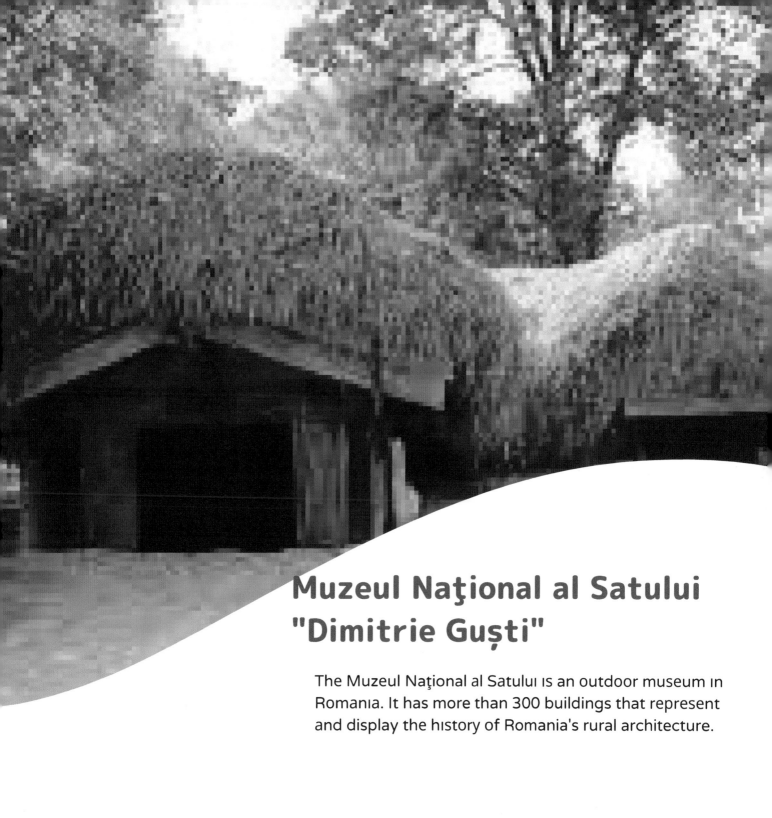

Muzeul Naţional al Satului "Dimitrie Guşti"

The Muzeul Naţional al Satului is an outdoor museum in Romania. It has more than 300 buildings that represent and display the history of Romania's rural architecture.

National Museum of Contemporary Art

The National Museum of Contemporary Art houses a collection of Romanian and Eastern European artists. It also contains some collections of new Romanian artists.

Food and Dining

Traditional Romanian food reflects the influence of Turkish, Slavic, Austrian, and Hungarian dishes. The dishes feature meat but also include vegetables, cereal, honey fruits, and dairy products. Soups made with meat or fish are usually common items and are usually the first course of the main meal.

Sarmale or Cabbage rolls stuffed with rice and spiced pork is regarded as the national dish and a favorite main dish. Other typical meals include Sausages and stews, Sawamura(salty grilled carp), and Muschi Poiana.

Accommodation

There should be little worry about accommodation in Romania because they are many no matter the season. Depending on your style and budget, you can choose from private rooms, hotels and pensions, cabanas, camping, village homestays, and youth hostels.

Transportation

The options for transportation are numerous. From trains to buses and taxis you are faced with quality options to travel around the country. Here are transportation options in Romania..

Bus

Taking a Bus in Romania is similar to every other European country. You'll buy a ticket from automated ticket machines or kiosks around the city, wait for the bus and stamp the ticket once you enter.

Car Rental

Car rental is available in Romania, but driving can be challenging and stressful because of the bad road network and high traffic.

Planes

Good choice for long-distance travel especially between Bucharest and Cluj-Napoca, Timișoara, Lasi, and Suceava. It's cheap, fast, and convenient.

Train

Train transportation is an excellent way to enjoy a stress-free journey. You'll see the beautiful views and the services are cheap and decent.

Maxi Taxi

Maxi Taxi is best for traveling across towns or remote areas on the outskirts of big cities. They are also a good option when train tickets are sold out, or the schedule is not convenient.

Light Rail

Romania has a broad light rail network for transportation. The light rail is more convenient than the bus since they have a larger capacity. You can use the same tickets for the bus and light rail.

Shopping

Shopping in Romania means buying standard European quality goods at lower prices. Bucharest, the capital city, is one of the best places for shopping in Romania. Most international firms and national stores are located there, especially on Magheru Boulevard. Typical things to buy include cosmetics, handmade wooden figures, textiles, glassware, porcelain, and traditional clothing. Before shopping in Romania, you need to convert to local currency.

When to Visit Romania?

The best time to visit Romania is between August and September. The weather is pleasant at these times, so you'll be able to tour wonderful cities and towns. It rains mostly between May and July, and the rest of the year is cold.

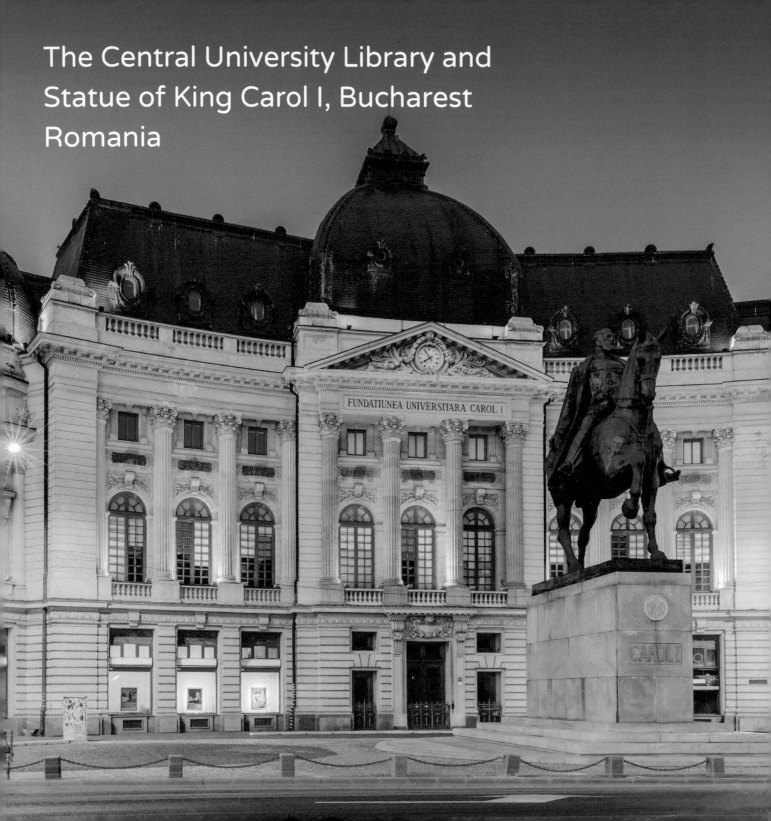

The Central University Library and Statue of King Carol I, Bucharest Romania

Printed in Great Britain
by Amazon

33303615R00025